In Focus

Sue Cook

In Focus

For John,
who has inspired many of these poems,
in one way or another, especially by towing
the caravan and me to poetic places far from home.

In Focus
ISBN 978 1 76041 086 5
Copyright © text Sue Cook 2016
Cover image: oil on canvas paper by Irma Denk

First published 2016 by
Ginninderra Press
PO Box 3461 Port Adelaide 5015 Australia
www.ginninderrapress.com.au

Contents

Family Snaps	7
An Ordinary Couple	9
A Quiet Poem	10
Life Unplugged	11
In Focus	12
A Riesling Affair	13
Frog Cakes	14
Time to Go	15
Leg Break	16
Daily Diet	17
For John	18
The Gift	19
Moving On	21
Drought	22
Paper Jam	23
Backyard Views	25
Elegy for a Koala	27
Takeover Bid	28
Blue Gums	30
The Visit	31
A Van Gogh Moment	32
Birthday Connections	33
Pot Plants	34
Hydrangea	35
Butterfly	36
Holiday Shots	37
Up the Murray	39
Melbourne 2007	40
Holiday Replay	41

Goolwa SA	42
Alligator Gorge	43
Willow Waters Gorge	44
Bogong Beat	45
Tag-a-long	46
Camp Abandoned	47
To the Island	48
Art Exhibition	49
Easter Odyssey	50

Focused Outwards — 55

Absence of Light	57
Clownery Suite	58
Detour	61
How to Listen to a Symphony Orchestra	62
The Market Gardener	63
Lost Shoe	64
The Comforts of Home	65
Hard Rubbish	66
Paradise	67
Cloaks and Mirrors	68
Meteorology	69

Acknowledgements	70

Family Snaps

An Ordinary Couple

Scarfed in silence they sat,
each in solitude
staring through the rain-mottled windscreen
at suburban vistas on either side
of the unravelling ribbon of road,
as the song of the violin
spiralled upwards from the radio
and the engine purred
propelling them forward
and then back into their humdrum life.
Here the scarf of silence slowly unwound
and the frictions of domestic discourse
rubbed against their solitude
still leaving her sidelined by his thoughts.

A Quiet Poem

For John

This is a quiet poem
for I have been shouting at you for years.
You have cropped white hair
and a generous girth
nurtured by your love of rich red wine
and only matched by your generosity of spirit.
You began working life in the army
where the firing of guns damaged your ears
so that later, teaching the mysteries of science,
if you couldn't hear a student's muttered answer
you just called on anyone who moved.
You are addicted to your computer, to emails, to forums,
because you don't have to filter the words through your ears.

On Thursday, we picked up a neat pair of hearing aids for you.
Yesterday for the first time I didn't have to shout,
I whispered I love you
and you smiled.

Life Unplugged

The band played on unplugged:
no electronic amplification
stripped right down
to acoustic instruments
a softer musical edge.

In our home I complain
that my husband is always plugged in to
hearing aids, headphones, computer.
But when he is stripped right down
to his naked ears and sounds are more than muted,
he is not so much unplugged
as untethered, in an acoustic world
just out of reach.

In Focus

The pink fairy is five and bounces
into focus
for the camera, wings adrift and tutu rumpled
from well meaning Christmas confrontations
of the physical kind –
she poses (camera whirrs) forever framed.
He is two-and-a-half and harder to snap,
blonde and boisterous
he grins at the lens
(or perhaps at some secret joke
he's unable to share)
while ripping the paper from another package.
These two invade our house this Christmas
borne hither by their parents on silver wings –
my daughter is mother and daughter
at the same time, not always compatible,
especially when she is wife too.
My mother died two years ago next month –
my own roles are different today –
mother, grandmother, wife and me.
I see my daughter so content,
I click the camera
and she too is framed
expecting her third.

A Riesling Affair

A one-wine woman
she had a two-glass limit
for the daily dinner.
Over the decades
rivers of cold Riesling
enhanced charred chops,
roast beef and smoked sausages.
On occasion, the tall green bottle
beckoned her at lunch,
its crisp palate
with floral overtones
made the humble sandwich
more attractive,
inviting a post-prandial nap.

One season the white grapes failed;
her Riesling rack was empty,
and in betrayal
she drank a mature, robust red
and was converted to its rich full body.

Now, she thought,
she could discuss the spicy fruit character
of a Merlot or Shiraz
with her husband and other red drinkers,
no longer a solitary white wine outcast.

Frog Cakes

Adelaide 1952

Seven excited girls, chattering loudly
like lorikeets at a feeder,
almost big enough to sit up to the best table
laden with mum's hearty home-baked birthday spread,
except for one daring, taste-tantalising plate
piled high with Balfours' frog cakes, iced in
garish green, Barbie pink and chocolate, in paper skirts,
square bodies with domed heads,
icing blob eyes and yawning cream maws.
Tempting beyond seven-year-old dreams of princesses kissing frogs.

Sixty years later I succumb again to frog cake fantasy,
an oddly Adelaidean concoction,
I rescue it from its supermarket shelf.
Secretly, I devour the pink frog cake
leaving the head till last as we did when we were seven.

But sadly the fantasy has been swallowed up by sensible eating,
nutritional rules and an ever expanding waistline,
the frog cake has become food for guilty thought.
I can't have my cake and eat it any more.

Time to Go

It's time to go, he said,
instead of soldiering on
for another long year
in the teaching trenches.

At his farewell dinner
friends brought packaged memories,
anecdotes, the familiarity of long association
and washed them all in fine wine.

At school sober speeches
accompanied a gargantuan glass platter
blue light reflecting through scribbled lines
artist's signature proving its worth and underlining his.

The question – what will you do – looms
but Christmas and holidays intervene.
Projects are lurking on the periphery of the festivities,
model boats, rotting decks and rafters, peeling paint,
projects that presuppose twenty less years.

But he's adamant – talking timber and paint
to his son the sceptic –
that it will just take longer,
he has all the time in the world.
To that other question – how do you feel –
he's not sure but thinks he will be smiling –
after all he's retired from teaching not life.

Leg Break

White on black
negative image
fractured bone.
Right leg sidelined
internal plate and pins
surgically implanted
in my right ankle
under spinal anaesthetic.
Numb from waist to toe
I am yet a watchful
listener at my operation.
A nurse takes my glasses
so nothing I can now see is
as hard-edged as the banter
of male medico voices
and the surgeon calling shot, shot.
I begin to imagine
I am forever trapped
in an episode of M*A*S*H
longing to escape.

Daily Diet

My husband devours the news,
he searches the record
for signals of discord
and other political clues.

My husband gobbles the word
empowered by Weet-bix
he relishes today's mix
of items seen, spoken and heard.

My husband digests the facts
of pestilence, famine and war
but indigestion arises the more
he consumes each daily tract.

My husband has eaten the news
from front to back and again
but in case his diet's still lacking
he tops up with television views.

For John

Long-lasting love is like a comfortable old shoe,
soft and well-worn it moulds itself
around the bunions of experience:
joy at the unfolding evolution of children,
grief at the early demise of parents,
financial crises, real and imagined.
It tiptoes around ingrained habits,
soft soles not disturbing
the consolation of deep familiarity.
Love's soft shoe shuffle.

The Gift

The odd shape,
encased in scarlet paper
clearly labelled Dad
gives nothing away.
He rips open the wrapping
reveals elegant wrought iron
a shallow ceramic dish.
He is delighted with the gift
but mystified,
until his daughter rescues him:
It's a bird feeder, Dad.

With love and hope he hangs the feeder
out the back, fills it with seed.
Bright green lorikeets, shy at first,
sample his offering, growing bolder,
argue about the pecking order.
Gawky grey and pink galahs try to land
but set the feeder swinging,
the dish and seeds scattered below.

He decides to make new feeders,
hangs these long stable troughs above the deck
fills them, awaits a response.
A raucous whirlwind of sulphur-crested cockatoos
plunges on the feast
rudely jostling, squawking, gobbling;
they ignore the opposition
perched in a hungry green row on the clothes line.

These confident cockies reap this bonanza,
heedlessly they plunder the offering
and greedily devour the gift
intended for all the birds.

Moving On

Bookshelves groan under the weight
of years of accumulated knowledge
in revelatory books and faded folders
of teaching wisdom.
Heavy with the gravitas of English literature
the folders loom above me like Damocles' sword,
daring me to peer inside and make decisions
about separation.
In the end I decide to jettison the lot,
save for a few meagre resources for someone else
who will no doubt rationalise them too
in the name of space.
The books find their own way home or to the library.
Meanwhile the boxes pile up in the corridor,
the shameful secret of their separation from me
revealed to passers-by.
My teaching life is packed and sorted,
no chance of a resurrection. Bridges burn behind me
as I sit at an empty desk, feeling the warmth
at my back.

Drought

I am like an empty dam with
my similes stuck to the bottom.
Words dry up and refuse to flow
as the heavens fail to open.
Level 4 word restrictions might conserve
what little poetry is left
but like the trickle from the hose
they inhibit flourishing growth
and limit output to the
meagre metaphors in the watering can.

No longer can I turn the drippers on
for the slow infusion of ideas.
Even my pen has dried up
as we await the deluge.

Paper Jam

Sentences slide smoothly
out of my word processor
through the printer
on to the paper
and abruptly end
when the error light flashes red.

I pull open the paper tray
certain it must be empty
to find instead my worst nightmare –
a menacing black cockroach
antennae quivering at the ready –
I scream,
rolled newspaper in hand,
'Death to all cockroaches.'
Those who live by the word
shall die by the word.

Backyard Views

Elegy for a Koala

Australia Day 2012

The blue gums creaked and groaned
under the lashing of the wind,
branches cracked and fell.
In the morning our breakfast guests
taking a morning walk,
despite the wild unruly weather,
found a lone dead koala
face down on the tinder dry grass
bookmarked by a broken branch.

But alas the unyielding rock hard
summer earth defeated
our fervent efforts
at digging his grave.

There were no funeral rites,
only a black shroud in an empty green bin,
his cortège a lone council garbage truck.
We knew not where this grim hearse would take him –
to the dump, a mass grave, a crematorium?
An ignoble end
to a national icon.

Takeover Bid

The honeysuckle fell
not with a crash
like a tree
but in a slow parabola
like a diver
arching backwards
into a swimming pool.

It subsided,
a tangled green mass on the front lawn,
as if Jack had attacked the Beanstalk,
when in fact John had been clearing the gutters.
Pruning the eager exploratory tendrils,
undercutting their takeover of tiles and woodwork
by such a savage severance
that the verdant structure
collapsed under its own weight.

Became exposed as a dead core
of tangled gnarled limbs
still generating new greenery,
tentative offshoots entwined unto the last.
Twelve years' growth eradicated in an afternoon.
The house trembled, naked and vulnerable,
until neat and tidy shade cloth
and tame pot plants
in manageable hanging baskets
restored its modesty.

But beneath the decking vigorous green shoots
enliven dead undergrowth. Productivity increases
as the honeysuckle begins regenerating,
increasing its shares
to boost another takeover bid.

Blue Gums

My blue gums are not polite –
rough, ragged and rude
they are forever undressing in the garden
in front of the neighbours and hapless passers-by,
littering the ground with curls of brown bark
like a teenager's clothes on the bedroom floor.
Indifferent to my welfare
they drop branches without warning
and sprinkle gum nuts on the driveway
just waiting for me to slip and slide.

Sometimes I yearn for more modest trees,
smooth and sensuous with graceful limbs
and white sculpted trunks,
a delicate crown that won't tumble down.

Still, it is the untidy tops
of my Tasmanian blue gums
that entice the local koala.
He doesn't mind their manners.

The Visit

We have had some unexpected visitors of late –
on the bird feeders flashes of red and green
announce the arrival of the greedy lorikeets
profligate with the seeds
which fall unheeded to the earth below.
Greenish-brown duck-billed visitors
waddle up the backyard or fly in
from the murmurous creek,
sometimes two, sometimes only one
as if to reconnoitre the territory for the other.
Spilt seed is the gourmet delight
with torn bread on the side
if we are quick enough.
They are shy and don't stay long,
just long enough to leave their calling cards in the grass,
the green, green grass.

A Van Gogh Moment

An unexpected tall visitor
appeared in the backyard today
growing between the felled blue gum trunk
and the faded red, straggly geraniums.
I spied her elegance from the house,
but she shyly turned her face away, sunwards.

When I drew close,
faced up to her with gentle greetings,
saw the radiant ring of yellow petals
fringing her fine black face,
I understood why Van Gogh
first painted sunflowers
for sheer joy in Arles in 1888.

Birthday Connections

A pearl-grey day –
rain misting down
muting the spring-green growth
in the backyard –
beyond the deck.

Grandchildren blow up balloons
bright dabs of colour
brushing the subdued setting.

Seats jostle in anticipation
of a throng of revellers
who arrive
coats, umbrellas, gifts, kisses
and find the party revving up
on the back deck.

Conversation creates bridges
spans sixty years
of connections,
sixty years of life.

Pot Plants

Sozzled by rain
bedraggled plants straggle over pots
and drip deckwards
dangling leaves of anaemic green –
where there are leaves left.
Some more drunk than others
appear drowned in excess liquid
but the cyclamen flaunts flagrant pink
over deep green leaves –
heralding the distant spring.

Hydrangea

On a long gnarled walking stick stem
a green furled tip, buds bursting towards spring
from brown concentric rings.
Venerable flowers, relics of summer past with
tossed and tangled petals, cream, dusky pink, nutmeg brown,
some dried and crimped as dead spiders.

Butterfly

Squeals of 'cockroach' pierce the afternoon air
and five anxious small faces retreat
from a black velvet package, clinging to the table.
No scuttling away, antennae waving,
this package just sits, gathering energy.
Straight from its cocoon it has tumbled
on to the table from the grapevine above.
Transported inside by careful curious hands
it is beginning to reveal its true colours,
white spots on black with a hint of orange.
We rescue it, take it outside, place on a leaf.
It clings, still hesitant about flying,
we watch, waiting in anticipation –
at last the butterfly unfurls its wings,
quivers,
and is gone.

Holiday Shots

Up the Murray

At Blanchetown, the 1956 flood watermark is 11.3 metres. In July 2010, the level of the river was 3 metres.

The houseboat, as big as Noah's Ark,
seemed unlikely to move anywhere, no floods today,
but we wallowed up the river
avoiding all the shallow bits.

In the dusk those who could, scrambled up the bank
and wrapped the mooring ropes
around some scrawny, sturdy gums.
As night fell the arcane male practice of finding wood
for a blazing bonfire on the bank was resurrected
while the age-old female ritual of conjuring food
was applauded by the men
as they downed beers
and watched the sparks fly
within and without the boat.

We awoke to find fingers of sunshine
lifting the veil of morning mist
and illuminating the holes in the golden cliffs,
homes to a commune of white cockatoos.
The rhythm and routine of lazy houseboat days
unleash us from the ties that bind us to home and work,
drawn into a new serenity
by the unfurling ribbon of the river.

As we motor slowly back to Blanchetown
a speedboat revs up through the silence,
knifing the Murray into smaller slices for future use,
river rations for all.

Melbourne 2007

In the hot breathless dusk of the backyard
a cricket ball lies abandoned
and a lone beach towel flaps on the line.
A sky of empty promises
darkens above the table
where the family lean into
and across each other
to share food and drink and talk.
Succulent steak sizzles on the barbecue
transforming later into warm beef salad
and the four cats wrap around legs
yodelling in anticipation
of their own more modest repast.

Early next morning as the heat hovers
there are intruders on the barbecue.
Two miner birds are pecking and tapping,
dancing and dodging,
making the most of the leftovers
and squawking their good fortune to others.

In the backyard
the cricket ball is recaptured
and the beach towel taken in,
ready for another long summer's day.

Holiday Replay

Melbourne beckons again
on the silver anniversary
of our first anxious parental visit to our daughter
who left the nest at twenty-two to work and live,
newly married, amidst the millions
of this teeming metropolis.

Today, their home explodes
with the joyful mayhem
of four exuberant teenagers and one excitable dog.
The fourth teenager has just survived the road trip
from Adelaide, long legs telescoped on the back seat.
An exchange student from Germany
she is eager to practise her English
and social skills, already well honed,
on our three grandchildren, and Ginger, the dog.

St Kilda beach, the Victoria Markets, Docklands,
our daughter is a happy tourist guide.
Back home the spa invites those under twenty
to test the water on this cool spring day,
while some of us over twenty raise our glasses
to the resilience of youth and Melbourne,
and our regular family holiday package.

Goolwa SA

September 2007

A disorderly platoon of ducks
marches web-foot up to the caravan
quacking like demented car horns
and crowds the steps in great expectation.
Its numbers swell
insistent bills thrust forward
tails waggling out of sync.
How are we to eat outside
with this chaotic chorus asserting
its territorial rights?
Resisting the brash blandishments
we retreat inside and withhold food,
hoping they will waddle off
to seek sustenance
from softer-hearted souls.
Later, I half expect to share
the showers with these assertive ducks
but they prefer the nearby river,
while it is still flowing.

Alligator Gorge

1 The Terraces

600 million years ago a beach was here.
I could have reclined on the warm sand,
absorbed the gentle sun and trailed an idle hand
in the cool water lapping on the ancient shore.
Now I tread awestruck over whorls and lines
in the rock, fossilised ripples of water.

2 Narrow Gorge

Feathery yakkas and spindly trees
cling to towering sandstone quartzite cliffs
and I hear water warbling over rock.
The creek is a translucent shade of tea.
An intermittent path beckons as it emerges
From the shadow of steep cliffs leaning inwards
and pressing relentlessly down.
There's no way out except forward,
back lies the daunting challenge of 250 steep steps
forward are the stepping stones in the creek,
slippery, uneven, angular, treacherous.

A woman with a walking stick
bravely wends a zigzag along the creek,
three children, insouciant, leap from rock to stone
fast disappearing into the distance at chasm's end.
I take a first tentative step in their wake.

Willow Waters Gorge

In the hush of the gorge
we sit on the horseback of a fallen tree trunk.
Ancient gnarled gums soar skywards
from the dry rock-cobbled creek bed,
tethered only by massive tangled roots
clutching to the trunks octopus-like
as if emerging from an unknown underground sea.
No beetling cliffs rise beside this gorge
but benign rounded red hills
define the course of the waterless creek.
Yellow wildflowers punctuate the grey-green bank,
as do two abandoned fire circles
made from plundered river rocks,
charred wood and oyster shells left behind.
Ancient silence surrounds us
>	except for
>	the whoosh of the wind
>	the whispering of the leaves
>	faint raucous cries from birds on high.

We might have been the first here
>	except for the fire rings
>	the oyster shells
>	and the flashes of brown glass in the dirt.

Bogong Beat

In the dark shroud of midnight
I thought I heard some odd sounds,
a kind of muted rat-a-tat
on the percussion skin
of the caravan roof.
Wake up! I said. Can you hear that?
A muffled no in response,
I rolled over, dreaming of rain pattering,
And thus soothed, I slept.

Rising early, I stepped outside
over the dead bodies
of a battalion of bogong moths,
abdomens full of eggs,
frantic wings folded now in peace.

Unwitting suicide bombers
they had detonated
against the roof
overnight. Their corpses now laid out
in serried rows before me:
Easy pickings for the birds.

Tag-a-long

In Merna-Mora in the Flinders
a motley assortment
of four-wheel drive enthusiasts and their vehicles
assemble for a long weekend of bush-bashing, barbecues and beer.
I'm not there.
But lots of adventurous people are
including my husband and our exchange student.
I am there
in the washing and the food bought before they left.
I am there
in the things that they forgot and I remembered
like hats, sunscreen and insect repellent.
I am assuming that they are there in the Flinders,
driving over rough steep outback tracks by day
and telling silly jokes by the campfire at night.
But I don't know.
They haven't rung. I believe they are out of range.
And I am here, at home, relaxing in the peace and quiet,
sitting in a stable armchair, not a rough and rowdy ute
bumping over creek beds and ungraded roads.

Camp Abandoned

In Johnburg sleepy bodies stirred
early on Sunday morning.
People listened, ears cocked,
to a drumming on taut canvas,
a syncopated rhythm on caravan roof.
Some drew back the tent flap and peered out
but in the cold wet darkness
the warm sanctuary of the sleeping bag beckoned.
At daylight the campers emerged,
as if from chrysalids,
onto red glutinous mud
pockmarked with rain,
soon to be imprinted with boots and tyre treads,
and oozing under tents and into every crevice.
We squelched across the campsite
packing up, no more exploring today.
Like rusty chewing gum the mud stuck to boots
and was trekked inside cars and caravans.
We took a bit of Johnburg home to Adelaide,
a Bendleby Ranges souvenir.
The rain stayed behind in the north.

To the Island

He put the Ford ute on the ferry to KI
for his seventieth birthday (I went along for the ride).
He flashed his camera through wind and rain
at Remarkable Rocks, climbing slopes with youthful tourists
(the Rocks no more remarkable than he, I thought)
and communed with seals clustering under Admiral's Arch.

At first at Seal Bay we thought we had missed the natives,
seeing only improbable trails in the sand dunes beside the boardwalk.
Suddenly, sea lions appeared on their sandy stage, flippering around,
flapping and flip-flopping, heads up, 'Look at *moi*, look at *moi*'
to rousing cheers from onlookers rugged up in coats and hats.
Too cold for swimming today, even for sea lions.

Food and warmth beckoned from afar, the local kiosk shut.
He grabbed the chance to put the ute into four-wheel drive
over the slippery unsealed road to Marron Café,
a gastro-haven in the middle of the island,
(marron thermidor for me).
When we clinked our glasses I forgot his seventy years,
seeing only the tall boy on his bike,
riding beside me to school.

Art Exhibition

The avant-garde artist who designed Central Australia
had a fondness for Lego
in unusual colours of red ochre, umber and grey.
She liked the way each block interlocked with the next
to make a pattern
and tried her hand on pimple hills
with ramparts on their crests.
Some of the Lego fell apart
toppling down the hills and dotting the ground
in the yellow, red and sage-green landscape.
But she was nothing if not persistent.
She gave up on the Lego and the arete
and turned to plasticine
moulding the Kata Tjuta
their breasts undulating against the distant horizon.
Still she felt the landscape was unfinished.
She mused and meditated
on the empty spaces
then tried papier mâché
in red ochre, grey and pink
fold upon fold upon fold
looming over the landscape.
At last she got it right, she thought,
at Uluru.

Easter Odyssey

1. Beachport

Abandoning Adelaide in the sweltering March heat
seemed like a good idea
as we headed for the south-east.
Salt flats and scrubby bushes marked the edge
of the Coorong in retreat
from an all devouring drought.
With everything on board the caravan,
including the kitchen sink,
we were ready to gently rough it.

Beachport loomed, a lazy languorous blue sea
belying the 41 degrees outside the cocooned
cabin of the car.
The caravan park clung to the beachfront,
caravans and tents jockeying for position
on parched grass under thirsty spreading trees.
Escape essential, we explored the town
greedily licking ice creams and looking longingly
down the endless jetty for the promised cool change.

2. Portland

In the park on the beachfront at Portland
the grass was lush and green, on all the vacant sites
sprinklers gushing water recklessly.
Ah, so we were in Victoria now. We set up camp
and negotiated a way through the black rocks
to the grey restless ocean, undercurrents tugging at the beach.

Later, snug in the caravan, we heard ominous gale warnings
and leapt outside in the driving rain to pull down the annexe
lest we become airborne and disappear out to sea.

On a lustrous day, earth shimmering after rain,
we donned backpacks, silly hats and serious walking boots
for the hike to Cape Bridgewater.
To reach the seal colony was an hour or more meandering walk
along the clifftop path where danger for fools lurked near the edge
of the precipice, ocean spray spuming over rocks far below.
Later, peering down from a cliff-clinging lookout
we spotted the seals, grey oysters slipping through the waves,
whimsical faces finally lens-focused.

3. Naracoorte Caves

We drove to Naracoorte on a less travelled road
through dense green trees, wipers steadily swishing,
until we set up camp to the cackle of kookaburras.
In the caves next day we exchanged daylight for darkness
and tiptoed tentatively into dark spaces;
calcium carbonate fingers strained to meet in sudden pools of light
and when the lights were extinguished for a breathless moment
I sensed the earth and concrete and trees above pressing down,
scrabbled upwards, such relief at reaching the surface.

4. The Return

At last, with the holiday folded back into the caravan
and the car hitched to our memories
we turned for home, swaddled by jazz
and sharing a sense of achievement
in surviving the caravan odyssey
and escaping the worst of the Adelaide heatwave.
Our hills home, intact, unburnt, still there, offered the final challenge,
backing the van down the steep drive
into the carport and us into long-forgotten routines.

Focused Outwards

Absence of Light

Like volcanic ash
darkness envelops me
seeping into every pore
with each fragment of daily news:
snippets of fear, hatred and danger,
glimpses of powerful politicians
intoning the morality of war,
through sombre images of soldier heroes,
some fallen, pursuing far-flung wars of attrition.

Windows into shattered lives of people
fleeing fire, flood and shuddering earth,
demolition of dwelling places,
the only sanctuary a hostile hillside.

Yet still shrouded in darkness
I turn off the TV and on screen
I see only my own reflection until –
in my inner dark something stirs –
a white shoot, tremulous, fragile,
reaching for light, for hope,
for that elusive change in the news.

Clownery Suite

1. No More Clowning Around

'Send in the clowns' – Stephen Sondheim, *A Little Night Music*

When the show is flagging
send in the fools, juggle the jokes,
milk the laughter with slick slapstick,
bulbous red nose on mobile white face
under iridescent green fuzzy-wuzzy wig,
a saggy baggy technicolour costume
and bespoke elongated shoes, made for pratfalls.

But where are they now?
Across the wide world there are news reports
of ageing clowns dropping out, dying,
disappearing from circus and stage,
leaving behind big shoes and baggy suits,
forsaking comic capers for pension cards,
and an audience who has forgotten how to laugh.

Who can we send in
now that world peace is flagging?
Send in the dogs of war –
nothing to laugh about.

2. Fear of Clowns

Clowns are disappearing
not from age alone –
their reputation's shot.
Some folks have a fear of clowns;
in Hollywood the seeds were sown
by movie bad guys like the Joker;
yesterday in town an armed woman,
clown-masked, was later shown
to be a crim with deadly intent.

In a fear-mongering world
how can sad clowns be funny
when their masks are no longer their own?

3. The Oldest Clown in Peru

Poverty encroaches on the margins
of bustling Lima, capital city of Peru,
where ten million people jostle for space
and a man may live until he's seventy-one years
if he's lucky.
Wave-lapped by the blue Pacific to the west,
overlooked by the perilous peaks of the Andes to the east,
Lima is home to Pitito, the oldest clown in Peru.

If clowns are on the endangered species list,
a dying breed, whose masks have been usurped by robbers,
as newspapers report,
Peru's oldest clown has not heard
nor taken heed of a melancholic media.
At ninety-one in his meagre home on Lima's fringe
Pitito still hones his circus skills,
studies an old dog-eared notebook,
nine richly remembered decades of clown jokes, riotous routines,
and a closet crammed with costumes.

Now when Pitito performs his routines
often his only audience is his adored wife, old too, but sick;
he dresses up, from fuzzy wig to floppy clown suit,
to hear her laugh is restorative for both.
He vows to keep clowning around
until death comes knocking –
even then he'll have the last laugh –
no coffin will be deep enough for his supersize shoes.

Detour

The road in front is closed
by barriers newly erected –
arrows indicate detour ahead.
I must follow the signs
driving up the hill
over the brink
and home to shelter.

As life decelerates
other detours lie ahead
but there are no signs to follow.
Climb the hill
over the brink
into the unknown
and beyond.

How to Listen to a Symphony Orchestra

A rare night out
concert tickets to the classics.
We ease into our seats,
I, a classical music novice,
can only hear a cacophony of sound
from the musicians on stage.
They're warming up, my companion says,
haven't started yet.

Sceptical, I reserve judgement…
the conductor struts on stage –
ripple of applause –
heartbeat of expectant silence.

Then the concert begins –
The musicians play with fervour
unfolding the shape of the music –
I hear the susurration of the strings
underscored by wailing woodwinds
bisected by bellicose brass
stamped with the precision of percussion
until, at last, avoiding fretful thought

I am swept along on
the tidal wave of music
to listen with joy,
surfing the tsunami of applause.

The Market Gardener

When my new neighbour came to live next door
he was a person displaced from his past.
For five decades he grew the best celery,
sturdy tall stalks with leafy green heads in refined rows
in the rich alluvial soil of the Brownhill Creek flats,
nourished by gentle flooding.
He chose the corner block here, empty ground, erratic creek flow,
still had a vestigial urge to create a market garden.
The hard clay suburban soil was less responsive
yet he grew prolific crops of vegies, never flowers,
hardy cabbages, carrots, onions, potatoes,
and his legendary runner beans.
His wife, her storage spaces shrunken,
often despaired of such abundance
and yearned for her generous kitchen overlooking
lush market gardens at Brownhill Creek.
She did not miss the early rising for market,
but he did, troubled and restless after 3 a.m.,
still tuned to the rhythm of that former life.

Time slowly encroached on our neighbours
and on the garden,
they each shrivelled and went to seed.
In the nursing home, they longed only for Brownhill Creek;
their suburban sojourn flickered dimly and died.

Lost Shoe

For weeks it seems
the shoe has sat on the junction box,
where tangled brambles
edge the dry creek
and the path through the grassy reserve
curves into the next street.
A right-foot sports shoe, high-top, with gold star,
jaunty pink, white and grey stripes.

Now gone –
perhaps it was a shoe acquired in a sale,
'BUY ONE PAIR OF SHOES GET ONE FREE',
left to languish in solitude
until a naked right foot
jumps in
and walks boldly forth,
blue sneaker on the left foot
trying to catch up.

The Comforts of Home

The streetscape of yellow-brown grass and grey-green gums
has surrendered its native dignity
for the dubious gentility of home discards.
Sagging armchairs and plump sofas in pink, blue and red
furnish the verges, jostling for space with rejected mattresses,
an invitation for lounging and lying around in the warm air.

The only layabout I see is a stern sepia ancestor,
formal coat and wing collar, trim moustache and beard,
dark eyes gazing rightwards out of a crooked frame,
demoted from his privileged position in the family gallery
to lean drunkenly against the stobie pole;
just another home discard
or a family portrait for a new wall.

Hard Rubbish

The verges are overgrown with other people's rubbish,
a fertile ground for scavenging where the scabs
are wealthy enough to bring their own trailers,
sifting, sorting and loading other people's detritus
and giving it a value way beyond its use-by date:
rubber tubing, metal constructs, a rejected lawnmower.
The exposed innards of family homes are left behind,
the nether side of the neighbourhood:
drawer-less desks, abandoned sofas, chair legs pointing skywards.
Ignored too are the rolled carpet and mattresses oozing stuffing,
a cot, a TV set, a swing and a bike broken beyond repair.
Half a surf board hints at pursuits beyond the prosaic
yet I want the verges back, that buffer zone between neighbours.
This hard rubbish collection is faintly embarrassing
like seeing other people's discarded underwear on display.

Paradise

Wet and cold, I was waiting at the bus stop
when a lumbering bus loomed into view
through the early evening drizzle,
its destination display PARADISE INTERCHANGE.
Damp and despondent I was tempted
to climb aboard, take my chances –

but surely it's too soon for my trip to paradise,
I'm not yet ready to join the celestial choirs,
and interchange is an unknown quantity,
what if it's the interchange to hell?

No – I'll wait for my regular bus
and be home in time for tea.

Cloaks and Mirrors

As I walk with care along the street
towards the magnetic shops
I see mirror images of my future self
hovering into view.
I recognise crumpled faces,
recycled clothes, sensible hats,
walking sticks, zimmer frames
and that particular rolling gait
heralding a hip replacement.

We smile tentatively
in mutual acknowledgement,
but from youth, no recognition;
we have acquired
the cloaks of invisibility.

Meteorology

Softly thrumming on the roof
the rain begins,
increasing the intensity of rhythm
just a little
as the drops plash down
in benign abundance
and drip from trees and pot plants
quenching the thirst of a long southern summer.
Abruptly, the rain stops,
a pallid sun fingers through grey cloud
and we look outside,
glad that the weather is as predictable as our lives.

In the north a cyclone gathers offshore,
the rain begins
increasing the intensity of rhythm,
a cacophony of sound
as the winds accelerate,
the trees bend and sway, are torn apart
as the rain and wind wreak havoc
as we watch the day's news.
Beyond quenching thirst this is sheer intoxication.

Abruptly the rain and wind pause for breath up north,
a raw egg sun struggles through purple cloud,
unsettled we stare at our TV screen
where the cyclonic images defy prediction
and complacency.

Acknowledgements

Friendly Street Reader
2000, In Focus; 2004, Time to Go; 2007, The Visit; 2012,
An Ordinary Couple (poem of the month, December 2012)
2013, Patterns of Living

Independent Weekly
A Quiet Poem, Butterfly

InDaily online
Hydrangea, Melbourne 2007, Elegy for a Koala, Winter
Knits, Lost Shoe, Frog Cakes (© Balfours, reproduced with
permission)

The Mozzie
Bogong Beat, A Riesling Affair, Up the Murray, Camp
Abandoned, For John, A Van Gogh Moment, Cloaks and
Mirrors, The Tenant, Detour

Positive Words
Willow Waters Gorge, Hard Rubbish, Blue Gums, Paper
Jam, Paradise, Tag-a-long

The Write Angle
Goolwa, Pot Plants, Drought, Art Exhibition

Spring Poetry Festival, Opinion 1988
Takeover Bid

Australian Poetry online *Sotto*
Alligator Gorge

Eureka Street online
Legbreak

www.ingramcontent.com/pod-product-compliance
Lightning Source LLC
Chambersburg PA
CBHW062154100526
44589CB00014B/1836